On The Edge

Scott Bulman
creator of
Wise Old Words

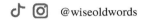 @wiseoldwords

ISBN: 9798481248325

Author's Note

Welcome to a safe place for my thoughts and feelings.

I've known exactly what it's like to be on the edge. I've experienced pain throughout my life including heartbreak, grief and depression, which can definitely be heard throughout these pages.

I began using social media to share some of the quotes that got me through hard times, which is where Wise Old Words began. After some time I started using my own voice through TikTok to project quotes which built a community of people who could also relate to these. Communication and expressing our feelings is one of the hardest things to do. When someone speaks up about what they feel or what they are going through, it's a reminder to others that they're not alone in their suffering and that in fact we're all dealing with our own hardships.

Throughout this book you'll find a short collection of deep thoughts, gentle reminders, quotes and poetry to motivate and inspire you while providing comfort and hope. My goal is to change the way people think and feel about themselves so that they want to take positive actions to lead to healing, self-discovery, inner strength, and personal transformation. I want this book to be a reminder that getting out of bed shouldn't feel like climbing out of a grave everyday. Life is tough, but so are you.

Thank you for allowing me to share a part of me. I hope to make at least one person in this world feel less alone.

Sincerely, a human. With feelings. Dreams. Ideas. Desires. And most importantly, flaws.

Scott

For all of my TikTok supporters.

We constantly find ourselves
worried we should have it all
figured out by now.

But there's no failure in
taking a little longer
to find your own way.

So don't stress about
scheduling your goals, you'll
reach them when you're ready.

Never
stop
seeking
moments
that
make
your
soul
come
alive.

The heart hurts because
it longs for the love it
cannot hold in the
present.

-Long Distance

Are you happy here?
Where the faces never
change and they all know
your name.

The road is open to those
brave enough to go beyond
what they know.

Don't settle when your heart
is tugging you forward into
adventure.

Be patient, your happiest
version of yourself is near.

You were the dry land I
needed to catch my breath
until the next flood.

But then I realised when
you use someone new as a
temporary fix, the ache
will always find its way
back.

Healing
yourself
is
your
greatest
revenge.

This is a letter to you:

The you that blames yourself when
something doesn't go to plan.
The you that feels invisible.
The you that doesn't know how
much longer they can carry on.

All these silent battles you're going
through right now and that aching
pain you feel in your chest are so
temporary.
The version of you in 6 months
time will be so proud that you
didn't give up.

Hold on.

It's okay to disappear for
a while to feel like you
again.

Someday everything will
make perfect sense.

I look at you now and
see that I never knew
you at all.

The worst part is now
you're just a stranger
that knows all of my
secrets.

Keep them safe darling.
I don't want the world
to know ways it can
hurt me.

Burn
me after
use.

No
second
chances.

It's
exhausting
isn't it?

Let it hurt,
then let it go.

Reminder: Having
boundaries for what you
tolerate in a relationship
doesn't make you
controlling.

Stop biting your tongue.
Blood will gather in your
mouth, slowly drowning
you.

Don't wear the mask for
too long.

Showing your pain is a
sign of strength.

So many of us
fear death... but
don't live our
lives.

Having anxiety and
depression is so hard
because you're in a
constant battle with
two completely
different demons.
And nobody
prepares you for
that.

Home
is
behind.

The
world
is
ahead.

I think I have spent too much
time trying to please everyone
around me and I was too scared
to talk or focus on my own
needs, which was the source of
so much pain.

This is your reminder, your
health and happiness should be
your top priorities. And you
definitely deserve to treat them
as such.

Stop fighting for
someone who is
okay with losing
you.

Being alone is the
upgrade.

The person you
want to be in
five years time
is so much
more important
than the person
you were five
years ago.

When your head hits
your pillow tonight,
remind yourself that
you are alright.
You are doing a
great job.
Be patient with
yourself and
remember big things
are achieved not all
at once, but one day
at a time.

Missing someone is
your heart's way of
reminding you that you
love them.

But remember, you can
miss someone and
continue letting go.

Don't ever hide your
anger.
Demand to be heard,
show them you are
serious.
You have the right to
feel emotions as deeply
as your body needs. And
the truth is, when people
tell you it's better to
stay silent, it's because
they fear your power.

Just imagine what's
possible once you let
go of the illusion that
it could have been
any different.

Pay attention to
the things you are
naturally drawn to.

The universe has a
path for everyone;
we just have to
have the courage
to follow it.

Lately i've
been
fascinated
by the sky,
because
it's all we
currently
share.

If you need
more time,
take it; this
is your
process.
Heal at your
own pace.

Some people
think that to be
strong is to
never feel pain.
In reality, the
strongest
people are the
ones who feel
it, understand
it, accept and
learn from it.

Bravery sometimes has
nothing to show for it
except survival.

Coming out alive is an
accomplishment they'll
never be able to take away
from you.

I'm ready to live
and I'm afraid that
includes letting go
of you.

You were content
here and I wanted to
see the world.

There's
someone out
there waiting
to make you
happy.

That someone
is waiting to
love you like
they would die
without you.

I promise.

Carry no more guilt
for the people you cut
off when they got
toxic.

Picking yourself up is
an act of resistance
when they forced you
down.

It's time
to learn
who you
are and
unlearn
who they
told you
to be.

Stop moving
mountains for
people who
can't even pick
a flower for you.

Nothing will ruin your
twenties more than thinking
you should have your life
together already. Deciding to
live on your own terms is the
most important decision
you'll ever make.

The goal is to embrace being
alone and start living your
life. The most important
person will always be *you*.

Slow down.

How beautiful is
it that someone
can make your
heart beat so
fast, even when
you don't want it
to beat at all.

One of the
hardest battles
you will ever
have to fight is
between who
you are right
now and who
you so badly
want to be.

Pretending
not
to
care
isn't
letting
go.

You're trying too
hard.

Don't exhaust
yourself by wasting
time on people who
won't move you
forward.

The past doesn't heal
and sticking with the
familiar won't let you
move on.

It's too late to
run.
You've already
invested
everything into
making this
work.

Never exactly knew what I was getting
myself into.
In the fell clutch of circumstance, I've
fallen when I least expected to.
Careless feelings bounded me to find
solace.
Over the years of my life you never knew
how much I long for your existence.
Losing you became my only fear and
trepidation.
Am I going insane.. but rather I feel finally
sane and finding self-actualisation.

You deserve people in
your life who think you
are a big deal.

No competition.
No backhand comments.
No jealousy.
No comparison.
No hate.

If I asked you what was
holding you back, would
you know it was yourself?

This is your life, you are
the only one able to make
it your best.

There is always room
for contentment, you
just have to find it in
every situation life
throws at you.

Likes, shares and
followers. Will any of
this even matter one
day?

Make sure you're
happy in real life and
not just on social
media.

I'm on a
journey that
will lead to
accepting
myself as I
am.

Believe in
your worth
so you'll
inspire
others to
discover it
too.

Wake up
every day
like it's
your first,
with
wondrous
curiosity.

Overreacting:
What people
accuse you of
when you call
them out.

You stuck by me.
You watched my pain.
You saw the parts of
me I kept hidden.
Yet you still chose to
love me.
Your patient soul took
the time to understand
my story and my heart.

Thank you.

Come out of hiding
and experience the
wonders life has to
offer.

You can't keep
waiting, the timing's
never going to be
perfect, so make it
happen now.

I found that
drowning is
the best
motivation
to learn
how to
swim.

If the world
ended while I
was looking at
you, I wouldn't
notice.

I hate it when people say
"life can't always be like
the movies"... Why can't it
be?

Go sing in the rain.
Go find your soul mate
and fall hopelessly in love.
Apply for that job.
Buy that plane ticket.
Move to that city.

You deserve a life you
can't wait to wake up to.
Never let anyone tell you
your dreams are
unrealistic.

Be the best you can
be no matter how
you're perceived; as
long as you're you,
no one gets deceived.

They may
not have
loved you,
but they
grew you.

Sometimes the
smallest step in
the right
direction ends
up being the
biggest step of
your life.

Tiptoe if you
must, but take
a step.

You're more
than you
think and you
don't need
recognition to
validate that.

I used to know you;
now it's like trying
to navigate an
unknown city
without a map.

In the end,
we will fall
into place
and it will
feel like
we're home.

I've always wondered
where I was supposed
to go.

No one could tell me.

I've been stuck here
as long as I can
remember trying to
get out, because i'm
scared of living a life
that was never meant
for me.

Even if you
let people
walk all over
you, they
will still
complain
that you are
not flat
enough.

There's really no
shortcut to forgetting
someone.

You just have to
endure missing them
everyday until you
don't anymore.

Strength
grows in the
moments
when you
think you
can't go on
but you
keep going
anyway.

Some
people are
in your life
to test you.

Never trust
your words
when your
heart is
bitter.

It's crazy how
someone can
break your heart,
but you choose to
love them with all
the little pieces.

Learn not to
give up.

*But to start
over.*

Freedom
is
being
you
without
anyone's
permission.

The best
days in life
are spent
carefree and
in love with
all of your
surroundings.

There will always
be a reason not to
do it, so do it
anyway.

Leap into this
with shaking
hands, buckling
knees and see
what happens.

Slow progress
is still progress.

You attract
what you're
ready for.

Being happy is a very
personal thing and it
really has nothing to
do with anyone else.

Reminder:
The circumstances
in which we might
fall in love are
rarely perfect.

The moment you
decide you want
better for yourself, is
the moment the
universe will begin
to shift in your
favour.

Somehow
our timing
was perfect.
What are
the odds of
someone
like you?

Don't let
excuses
become so
common
that you
begin to
accept
them as
the truth.

Even though right
now I don't know
where i'm going,
i'll walk anyway.

Stop looking for
happiness in the
same place you
lost it.

It won't be easy,
but I promise it's
possible.

I
want
to
heal
from
the
things
I
don't
speak
of.

Don't be
discouraged,
breaking is
the easy
part, now
you build
again.

Remember
to refocus
your energy
on healing
instead of
revenge.

We must
challenge
ourselves to
step out of
our comfort
zone on a
constant
basis.

People think being
alone makes you
lonely, but I don't
think that's true.
Being surrounded by
the wrong people is
the loneliest thing in
the world.

In the end, we
only regret the
chances we
didn't take,
relationships
we are afraid
to have, and
the decisions
we waited too
long to make.

Time always
exposes what
you mean to
someone.

Sometimes you just
need to take a step
back and realise how
far you've come
instead of how far
left you have to go.

The greatest
mistake you can
make in life is
to continually
be afraid you
will make one.

If it is poisoning
you, then it is not
love my dear.

It's not
guaranteed to
work out.

But maybe
seeing if it does
will be the best
adventure ever.

This is not weakness.
It's simply a minor
setback that you now
get to *grow* from.

It's crazy how
one drop of
love can create
a sea of tears.

Every
new
day
is
another
chance.

I feel as though
I've picked up the
pieces so many
times. I've taken
that leap of faith
and risked it all,
but now I just want
someone to jump
and reach for me
before I go under.

You are my
home, but
we're built
on unstable
ground.

You could map out the
most ideal environment
to be surrounded with,
but if you're not all in
with yourself, you're
not going anywhere.

We don't keep
moving because
we want to, but
because the
universe within
us wants to pull
us forward.

Don't anchor
yourself to your
suffering.

Being broken
taught me far more
than I could have
ever learned whole.

While the concept
'abandon hope'
might sound
depressing and
pessimistic, in
truth it's honest
wisdom learned
from years of
experience.

I carry the
weight of
so many
things that
weren't
mine to
hold.

The truth is,
when we are
hurting we
don't go to the
happy people,
we look for
the suffering
ones just like
us.

There is a whole
world in you to share
with others, and the
most important person
you can offer all of
that to is yourself.

Love yourself fiercely
and in doing so show
them how they should
treat you.

They say it gets
better, time
softens the
blow, but it's
been months
and it still
knocks the
wind out of me.

I don't really believe in
much these days. But,
one thing I know for
sure, hell is real and
you dragged me there
every chance you got.

Facing
disaster
will
help
you
overcome
your
insecurities.

People think i'm
bitter for
assuming the
worst out of
every situation,
but the more I
 prepare myself,
the less it will
hurt.

I admire the
effect of
good music.
It has the
power to
make you
forget or
remember
everything.

Be your true
self, because in
the end that will
always pay off.

Reminder:
Forgiving someone
who hurt you doesn't
make you weak.
Allowing yourself to
look past the pain
they caused you is so
powerful.

Never
lose
yourself
just
because
you
found
someone
else.

Take this as a sign,
the one you've been
waiting for.

Printed in Great Britain
by Amazon